In The Land of Cotton

By: Dolly O'Dell Williams

Photography by:
Bart Williams
Amanda Williams
Caroline Williams

DollyWilliams@Copyright2015
ShadesCreekPress.LLC@Copyright2015
Shades Creek Press, LLC
Savannah, Georgia

First Edition
First Printing, 2015

Book design by Dolly Williams & Natasha Walsh
Cover design by Natasha Walsh

Proof-reading & editing by Candice Lawrence

In The Land Of Cotton
ISBN: 9780000000
Copyright@2015 Jesse R. Hale
Shades Creek Press, LLC

Printed in the United States of America

The farmer pulls a plow over the field to loosen the soil. A new crop year has begun!

The ground is being prepared for spring planting.

The farmer tries to make the rows as straight as possible.

The seed is small and covered with a powder to help it sprout in the ground. The seed needs water, sun, good soil, and the right temperature to start growing.

Once the seed germinates, or sprouts, it will try to push the two seed leaves through the soil.

The cotton plant can grow very quickly.

As the plant grows, it will begin to bloom.
The blooms that are white have opened today.

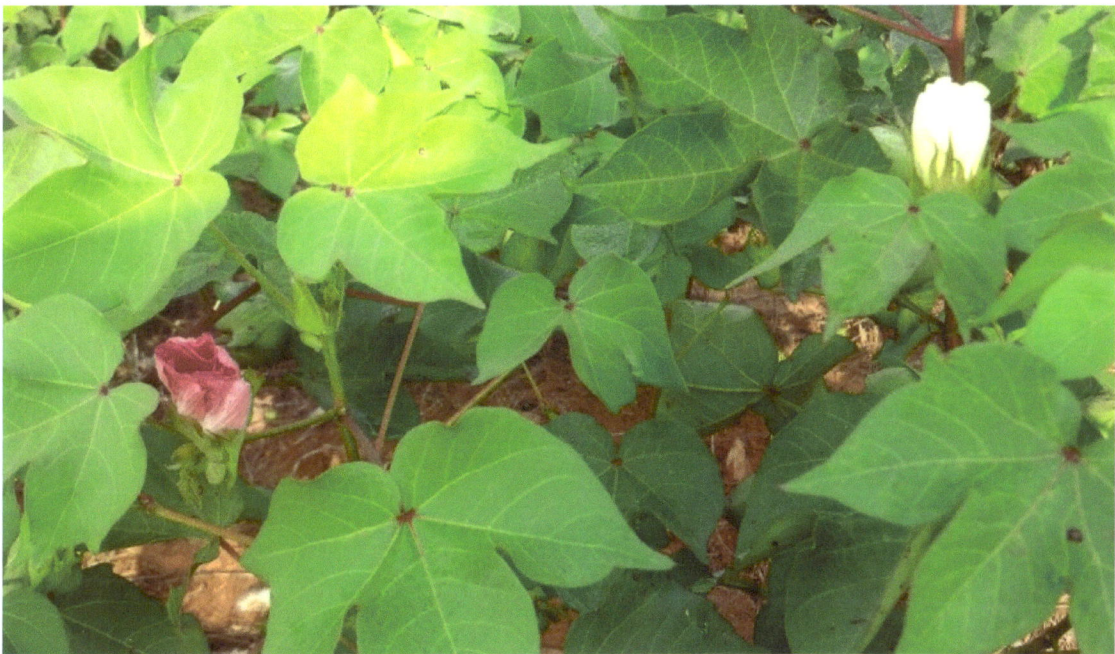

The blooms that are light pink to dark pink opened yesterday. The blooms mean that a baby cotton boll is on the way!

Behind each bloom is a "square", which really looks like a funny triangle.

The cotton plant will try to grow while putting a square on each limb or stalk of the plant.

The cotton squares are the beginning of the cotton boll.

The farmer watches out for worms, moths, and other pests that may damage the cotton boll. He will "scout", or look at his cotton several times a week.

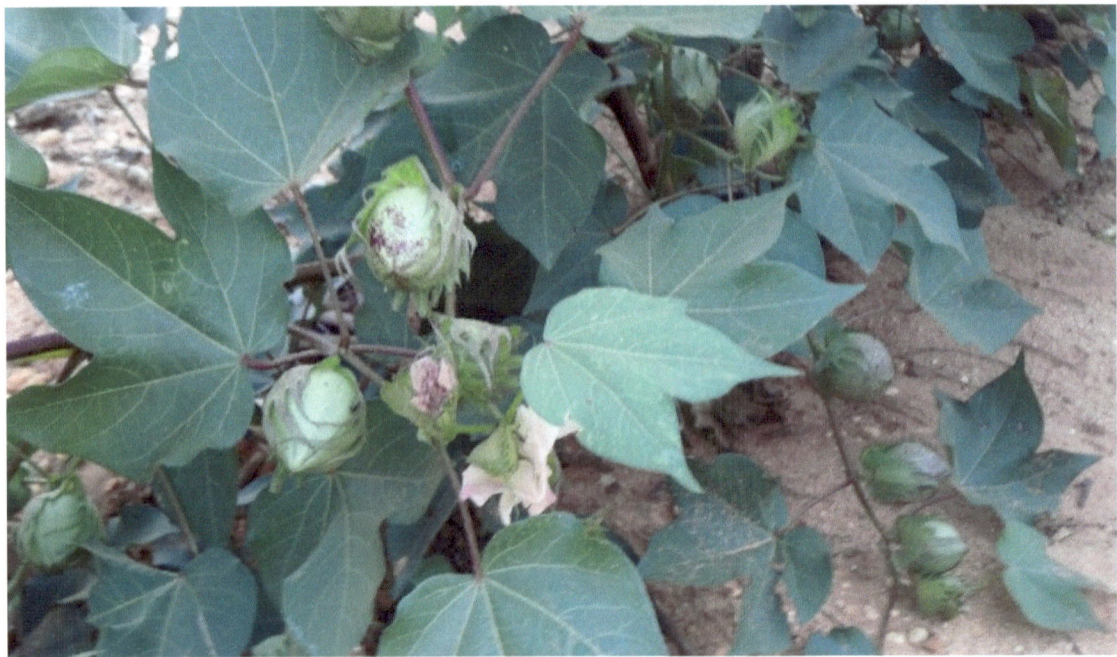

These cotton plants are loaded with bolls! The farmer is hoping for a good harvest when he picks his cotton.

Sometimes the farmer will need to spray his cotton. He can use a "high boy" like the one in the picture or have his field sprayed by a plane called a "crop duster".

The farmer will spray his crop with a product that helps "defoliate" the cotton. The defoliate makes the leaves fall off and opens the bolls.

The defoliate is beginning to work.

A boll with five sections means the possibility of a good crop!

These fields are ready to be picked. Harvest time!!

The cotton is white and fluffy. It should "pick" very well.

This is a "4 row" cotton picker. This means that it can pick 4 rows of cotton at one time. There are larger machines that can pick more rows. The picker basket can hold 1 or more bales of cotton. A bale of cotton weighs around 500 lbs.

When the cotton picker basket gets full, a worker will drive a tractor and machine to the cotton picker in the field. The picker will rise up and pour the cotton into a machine called a "boll buggy". The boll buggy driver then takes the cotton to the module builder to be packed.

At the edge of the field is a machine called a "module builder". This machine will pack the cotton. The boll buggy dumps the cotton into the module builder.

The workers will pack the cotton very tightly into a "module" or brick of cotton. They will pull the tractor away from the module and cover it with a tarp.

Once the cotton field is completely picked, the farmer will tag the module and call the cotton gin. The cotton gin will send a big truck to the field to pick up the module. This "module truck" slides under the module and takes it to be ginned. One module may have around 18 bales in it.

The cotton gin will separate the seeds from the cotton fiber. The cotton fiber is packed into bales, weighing around 500 lbs. The farmer is now ready to sell his cotton crop.

Thankful for a good crop, the farmer cuts the cotton stalks during the winter. In early spring, the fields will be ready to plow and prepare for another crop year!

Be sure to thank a farmer for the food and fiber that they provide for all of us!

A special thank you to Levi and Dan Gaines for allowing us to photograph their operation.

www.ingramcontent.com/pod-product-compliance
Lightning Source LLC
Chambersburg PA
CBHW042007080426

42733CB00003B/34